mending

a collection of poetry and prose

christina

christina valles

mending

mending

Printed in the United States of America.

ISBN-13: 978-1981290123
ISBN-10: 1981290125

Edited by: Lori Cook
Cover art by: ©jemastock, ©m.kucova, and ©grmarc via Canva.com

dedicated to all those who never believed in me

who tried to convince me that my dreams

were unrealistic

your words did not discourage me

they instead did the opposite

thank you for giving me the motivation

to prove you wrong

christina valles

<u>contents</u>

christina valles

i.

needle

my mending

here i open up to you
every last crevice of my mind.
the parts i've kept hidden for years
the ones i never dared to speak of.

my success
and my failure.

my experiences with falling in
what i thought was love.

being in toxic relationships.

my journey of turning self hate
into self love.

heartbreak
heartbreak
and more heartbreak.

losing myself only to later
find myself.

my mending.

beauty in simplicity

one may say my poetry
and written words
are too simple
or not profound enough.

but i believe it is simplicity
that we need to be reminded of.
that we need to learn
to find comfort in.

majority of the time
the most important things
the things we do not appreciate enough
the things we often take for granted
are the simple ones.

muse

it's true what they say,
you know.

to be cautious when loving an artist.

the painter will turn you into a masterpiece.
thinking of your eyes as they dip their brush
into the chocolate brown acrylic paint
recalling how intricate you are
within each stroke they make.

the musician will turn you into a melody.
one they simply cannot seem
to get out of their head.
the one which forms after hearing your laugh
and voice sweet as honey
only wishing to one day
make a song as beautiful
as you.

the writer will turn you into a poem.
one in which they use
every last word they know
to string together the slightest idea
of how you make them feel alive.
constantly wishing there were
more words in the English language
because no matter what they do
there are never enough to describe
the depths of you.

it seems like a dream,

to be somebody's muse.
but it can quickly turn into a nightmare
if you break their heart.

you would think they would want
to wipe you from their memory.
instead they will use the pain
way more than they ever used the love.

the once soft,
gentle brush strokes
will become unforgiving ones
as the painter curses your name
with each that is made.
ones so hard that the brush begins
to fall apart
and leaves the canvas covered in more than just paint
but with dents and rips as well.

the once soothing lullaby
they saw you to be
that could easily help you
drift off into a deep sleep
will become a song of terror
that keeps you up at night.
it will have a rhythm you can only
beg to leave your mind
even though it is already stuck with you forever.

the once rose scented love letters
you received every Sunday afternoon
will become tearstained letters of
heartache and despair
leaving you to wonder how something so simple

as words on paper
can hold the power to break you.

because it is pain
that keeps an artist going.
it fuels them as if it's their gasoline
and here you are,
adding fuel to the fire.

because it is the pain they use
to turn something once so hurtful
into something beautiful.

how else do you think
they cope with their problems?
why else do you think
they spend hours locked away in their room
finalizing their art?

so i warn you,
be cautious when loving an artist
because you may soon realize
you would much rather enjoy
viewing art
rather than
being the art.

but it will be too late
because they have already made you
immortal
through their art.

observation

i want to familiarize myself
with you.

i'll count each freckle
that dusts your face
and study the way
your eyes glitter
when you stare at the sky.

i'll notice how you can
never leave the house
without your lucky socks on
and the pattern your nose
scrunches up into
when you hear a joke.

i want to discover
parts of you
in which you
don't dare tell anyone
and the ones
that you didn't even
know existed.

morning routine

find someone who wakes up
ten minutes earlier
than need be
just so they can brew up
a warm cup of coffee for you
remembering that you add
three spoonfuls of sugar
and puts in a little kick of espresso
on the days where you
work till six.

find someone who wakes up
with you being the
first thought on their mind.

electricity

i ached to be in your arms
and almost as if
in some far off universe
my mind spoke to yours,
you laid your body close to mine
wrapping me in your embrace
your fingers against my skin
sending a rush through me.

a rush
meant to spark something.
a rush
meant to connect two people
into one.

i hope you felt it too.

the magic minute

it's 11:11
and i wish for you.
your sweet tasting lips
colliding ever so gently
against mine.

it's 11:11
and i wish for you.
your strong yet
such gentle hands
intertwining with my fingers
like a puzzle
that was begging to be solved.

it's 11:11
and i wish for you.
the freckle on your cheek
that you despise
and i can't help
but love.

it's 11:11
and i wish for you.
i wish that
you're wishing for me too.

trust

you have me in the
palm of your hand.
i constantly long
for your touch
and affection.

don't crush me.

exploration

you are the map
with all
your twists
and turns.

leading me
straight back to where
i'm meant to be.

i want to explore you.

be careful when playing with fire

you'll soon meet someone
who ignites a fire
inside of you.

be cautious
to not let them
burn you out.

simple complexities

i've always loved the little things like being able to sleep in an extra 10 minutes or having a fresh warm blanket to hug me during a rainstorm. i love a glass of ice water after laying out in the sun and when a song i haven't heard in years comes on while i'm inside a store. my whole life i've been a fan of simplicity because difficulty scared me, until i met you.

you were the most complex human being i've ever encountered, from the scars on your face to your reasoning of why you aren't so fond of romance movies and your standoffish personality that only lured me in more. you were a book waiting to be read and if only you knew how much i enjoyed reading.

it wasn't until after i learned to love you that i realized there are no such things as difficult humans, but instead humans who are made up of millions of simplicities that form us into who we are, waiting to find someone who is willing to take the time and explore each one.

infatuation

i do not want to be known to you
as just another pretty face.

i want you to be intrigued by my thoughts
and amazed with the way my brain works.
where all you want to do is listen to me ramble
to the point where you wouldn't
even need music anymore
because my voice has now become
your favorite melody.

i want you to be in awe
with my creativity and talents.
having you stare at me wide eyed
jaw dropped
not from my looks
but from a poem of mine you read
leaving you in complete wonder
of how i am able to
use words to fill your
once black and white world
with color.

i want to leave you left to ponder
how you ever even thought
others compared to me.
i want to change your perspective on life
sharing my past experiences with you
and you sharing yours with me.

we will use the mixture of both
to create our new experience

together.

i'll have you grow an obsession with clocks
because you'll spend all your time
counting down the seconds
until the next time you see me.

i want to leave an impression on you,
a mark you cannot rub away
i want you to become infatuated with me.

033098

it was my birthday
when you told me you loved me.

instantly i froze
and no words were able
to leave my mouth.

the words comforted me,
but also brought about
a familiar fear.

as the last time
someone told me this
soon after

they left.

secret love

i have never been able
to properly explain
the love we have.

it does not seem possible
there are no words
to do it justice.

there is no way
to create a sentence
that would give off
even a hint
of what we have.

it is something
that only you and i
will ever know of.

it is one of a kind
and it is ours.

you 4 you

i realized i loved you
not when you were dressed
in your Sunday best,
but instead when you wore
that old wrinkly gray tee
you refuse to throw away.

i realized i loved you
not when you were freshly shaved
and wide awake,
but instead when you hadn't
groomed yourself in days
and mumbled your words
as you rubbed sleep from your eyes.

i realized i loved you
not when you ate carefully
as others were around,
but instead when you dropped
crumbs onto your legs and
had food stuck to your chin.

i realized i loved you
in those real moments
that made you
you.

love me fully

when you say you love me i hope you're including all my flaws, not just your favorite features of mine. when you say you love me i hope you mean you'll love me when i'm crying on the bathroom floor, not just when i'm beaming with happiness. when you say you love me i hope you continue to love me even when i make it hard to do so, because to you, loving me is easy. when you say you love me i hope you love me all the time, not just when it's convenient for you. when you say you love me i hope you truly mean you adore every single last part of me.

or else you don't love me.

eternity

you have my heart
you have my soul
all of it is yours,
yours to hold.

for as long as we live
until we perish.

i hope you take good care of it
as it's yours to cherish.

my endless reverie

your glittering eyes
give me a sense of hope
i could look into them
until sunrise.

your character
is one i wish to explore
and know deep down
all the way to its core.

your heart warming hug
is one i could feel forever
it cures all of my worries
it's my everlasting drug.

your sense of humor
makes my stomach ache
from all the laughter
i haven't felt in ages.

i hope to never awake
from the dream
of being yours.

yellow

you remind me of the color yellow. i've always loved that color, despite how underrated and overlooked it is. it's the color of sunflowers that fill a field, with not just an immense amount of life, but with a reminder of how pretty simplicity is. yellow is the color in which the sun shines, lighting up your eyes to reveal their true power to win me over with just one look. it's a feeling. i like to say when i get that bubble of happiness inside my stomach, that i feel yellow.

to me, you're my yellow.

you're someone who surprised me with your ability to make me *feel*. it didn't take long for me to be wrapped around your finger, completely mesmerized by you. you're someone that helps me remember love can be found in hand holding, late night phone calls and cheek kisses, all the things we tend to not even think twice about. it can be found where some forget to look and where others don't even bother to check. you remind me that love happens when we least expect it.

timeless

i still remember that early morning
when we sat on the
parking garage rooftop
watching the sun swallow the world.
you didn't know i had my eyes
mainly fixed on you.

and as the yellows and pinks
the sunrise portrayed
turned into a
clear baby blue
i felt my heart stop for a second
as i remembered all beautiful things
will at one point
come to an end.

without even thinking twice
i leaned over and held you
a bit tighter.

hoping that if one thing in this world
were to last forever
it would be us.

itchy sweater

please never look down on yourself
for how hard you love.
it may at times seem
as if you're too much
you might even compare yourself to an ocean
but there is nothing wrong
with surrounding someone in love.

some people are still learning
how to love themselves
accepting it from someone else
feels foreign.
the idea itself is unknown
and the feeling has never been felt.

you must be patient
with those who are new to love
it is so important to show them
how deserving they are of it
not only from you,
but from themselves.

do so carefully
always keeping your best interest
in mind
do not allow yourself
to become lost
while trying to find somebody else.

your love will feel like
an itchy sweater
they'll be so focused on the

uncomfortability
they will tug
and stretch it out
they will curse under their breath
and throw it
on their bedroom floor
not ever taking time
to realize
it was keeping them warm.

young lovers

i think the reason why so many young lovers fall away from one another is because before they come together, they do not realize both are still in the process of growing. they expect the most of someone when both have not even discovered all of the potential within themselves. yes, we continue to grow until we take our last breath on earth, but i think the majority of it happens while we're young. with so many fast paced changes happening as you crossover into the world of being an adult, you go through what seems like the never ending process of finding yourself. when you fall in love with somebody going through the same thing, it makes the love ignite. it creates a love that is passionate and lights up your world, but many forget to realize when something ignites, it has the ability to burn out at any second. you have the choice to pursue the flame, or completely destroy it.

growing with someone is difficult, especially when you are both trying to find yourselves. it is crucial to remember you must keep your growth as an individual separate from the growth within your relationship. if not, you end up believing the other person is needed for you to grow, when that is not true. people can help you grow, but they don't *make* you grow. no one can fill your emptiness, and when they leave, even if it hurts like hell, you are capable of being full on your own. this stays consistent when you keep your self growth in a separate category than your relationship growth.

when you are able to grow a relationship as its own special thing, it will live to its full potential. when you communicate and work out each problem, instead of always resorting to, 'let's just sleep on it' or being too stubborn to hear the other person out, the bond will grow stronger. when you recognize you are two different people, who think differently, who feel differently, who *love* differently, you will learn to appreciate viewing life from another person's eyes, instead of belittling them for not thinking like you. when you understand that any relationship is able to last forever if you put in the effort, work for it, and ache for it, then your fire will never burn out.

concrete

my whole life i've kept up walls
i wanted them to be
indestructible.

as time went on
the walls became
stronger
only making it more difficult
to let anyone inside.

while putting up these enclosures
i didn't realize i wasn't only
locking out intruders
but i had made it impossible
for me to get back inside.

the rock solid walls
kept me locked out
from my true self.

nocturnal

my fear of sleeping emerged
after the consistent nightmares
that i could no longer
push through.

you'd think with how much time
i now spend awake
i wouldn't be so afraid
of living.

1 vs 1

there is nothing scarier
than your own mind
being against you.

what are you meant to do
when you're trying with all you've got
to save yourself
even though at the same time
you're running until you're out of breath
away from yourself.

short circuit

i was so busy trying to be
the light
in others lives,
focused on being
the sunshine
in human form,
putting their needs above my own,

i never stopped to realize
my own light
was dim.

half full

how do i come to terms
with the fact
you'll never be mine
as i spend my nights
trying to express my feelings
through heart filled rhymes.

how do i go about seeing you
give yourself
completely
to another
who doesn't even
love you deeply.

absence

and just like that
you were gone.

but this time
you didn't leave
a kiss on both my cheeks
and one on my forehead.

you didn't leave after
embracing me
filling my body with an energy
that made me feel invincible.

you didn't tell me
to text you when i had
returned home safely.

you didn't say
"i'll see you soon".

you just left.

spurious tellings

i told myself i was over you
yet the first thing i did
when i woke up
did not include
stretching out my limbs
or eating a hearty breakfast.
i did not at first
brush my teeth
or let the dog out.

instead i pulled up
our old messages
and read them
like the morning paper.

i told myself i was over you
even though for some reason
before i left for the day
i put the spare key back
in its secret spot
that only you and i know of
just in case you decided
to return home.

i told myself i was over you
but in the car the playlist i chose
for my journey
was titled *ours*.
the memories came flooding back
with each second the music played

and even though the beat

was steady
it left me feeling
unbalanced
as if the road was broken ice.

i told myself i was over you
but it didn't matter
how many times
i said those words
because i knew i was still wrapped up
in the thought that
maybe one day
you'd come back.

closed doors

i opened up to you
and showed you
my insides
but suddenly
you left without
saying goodbye.

i was stuck to ponder
what i had done
to all of a sudden
make you wander
away from me
to someone else.

had i told you too much?

should i have kept quiet?

you would have still stayed
without a doubt.

and you see, this is why
instead of
opening up
i shut people out.

shout into the void

you're scared
you do not want to
be left in the dust
you don't want to be set out
only to just rust.

can you not see
that i am the one for you
and you are the one for me?

you distancing yourself
breaks me inside
i feel as though
you are leaving me behind.

what have i done
to make you move onto her?
what can i do
to make you return?

puppet master

i thought the only way
to prove my love to you
was by allowing you
to walk in
and out of my life
as many times as you pleased.

every time you came back
deciding to finally give me
the time of day
i would tell myself,
let him in.

i gave you
complete control over me
without ever even noticing.

drowning

i always viewed you as
an ocean of love
pulling me in
wave by wave.

they were not calm
or easy going
but instead each one crashed
right into me
knocking me down.

i soon realized
i was not able to stay afloat.

i was drowning.

your love was not supportive,
but rather suffocating.

note to self

isn't it odd how much love
we put into those
who do not give even
an ounce of it back?

maybe we see a bit of
ourselves in them.
you think back to the time
where you were unable to love
no matter how badly you wanted to.

maybe we don't recognize
how much we deserve.
you're still in the process
of learning your self worth
that you've decided to settle for now
rather than putting that love
into someone who feeds it
right back into you.

maybe we're too scared
to be alone.
it doesn't matter if you
end each night
soaking your pillow with salty tears
because you'd rather have someone there
even if they are not worthy of you
even if they are draining the life out of you
at least someone's there.

maybe we're too busy
making excuses

and writing poetry about them.
because when you write about them
you can make them
whoever you want them to be
you can make them love you
the way you wish they did
you can create a story
a dream
out of a nightmare.

incomplete

i make it a habit to
preach kindness
with whomever i encounter
i do my best to help them
love themselves.

seeing anyone speak
harsh words
against their own being
breaks me inside
and i do all i can
to give them pieces
allowing them to
put themselves back together.

maybe that's why
i feel so incomplete.

i have never taken
one of my own pieces
or taken
my own advice.

i'm stuck constantly
in the same state
of emptiness.

black ash

my worst nightmare
has learned how to
disguise himself.

instead of showing his true intentions
right off the bat,
he now starts by taking me
gently by the hand
with a charming grin
along with a sparkle in his eye
that makes me believe
he would never
do anything to hurt me.

he relights that
fire inside of my soul
illuminating a pathway
straight to my heart.
the one i've always
lacked a match for.
convincing me i'm able to provide
the same fire for him
to be his everlasting warmth.

but soon enough
my fire is blown out
by the same person who lit it.
only leaving me with
black ash
and smoke that tastes of him.

blind

you gave me warning signs,
yet i pretended like they weren't there
you told me you weren't
good enough for me

and weren't worthy of my love

but i'd assure you
that you were.

i'm not sure if i repeated it so much
in hopes to convince you
or myself.

you told me i deserved better
i wasn't in a strong enough
place at the time
to realize you were right.

so now can you see
why i don't fully blame you,
but rather myself.

i broke my own heart
trying to heal yours.

differences

the difference between
you and i.

i saw myself waking you up
with soft kisses
on a Sunday morning
wrapping myself around you
admiring all your features.

you saw yourself in my bed
touching my body
on a Friday night
with not one thought of me
only of yourself.

i wish you would've
made the difference clear
before luring me in.

flowers on the floor

you made me feel special. as if i was the only one who had hands capable of holding onto your heart. as if i was the only one who held the key that unlocked your deepest secrets. as if i was the only one who could make you smile. that *real* smile. the one i thought only i was seeing.

except i didn't realize the same toothy grin you were giving me was the one you won her over with when you introduced yourself. i didn't realize the parking garage rooftop you took me to where we started off our mornings watching the sunrise was the same rooftop where you ended your nights watching the sunset with her. i didn't realize the reason why the fire inside of you was never ending was because she would be relighting it on the days when i wasn't there. i didn't realize the "forevers" you were telling me sounded so perfect because you already had practice saying them. i didn't realize the flowers you were putting in my hair were the same ones you picked up off her apartment floor after she stomped them to the ground when she found out about me.

despite all of this, what took me the longest to realize and what i still struggle coming to terms with, is that i was never special to you at all.

new eyes

i loved you so much
enough to replace
my eyes
with two new ones.

ones that didn't see
the anger
which filled your face
when i couldn't be who
you wanted me to be
and was then poured onto me
like scorching hot water,
but i made myself believe
it was a good kind of burn.

ones that didn't see
how much respect
you would give to whoever
didn't resemble me.

because according to you
i didn't deserve anything
except a cold shoulder
and a reminder of how
little i am to you.

ones that didn't see
your mistakes
because i knew you were human
and they are inevitable.
except for me
i was expected to never once

make a mistake
i was expected to be perfect.
ones that didn't see you
with her.
or her.
and her.
instead of running away
i'd run right back to what i thought
was home.

but home isn't supposed to make you
feel unwelcome.

ones that didn't see
your lips
and the pattern they moved in
when you would shout out
how you never once cared
and have never
loved me.

because my new eyes
never saw the warning signs,
despite how many there were.
never saw the
pain i was feeling,
as i cried until i fell asleep each night.
never saw the wrongdoings,
which occurred on a daily basis.

they only saw
what i wanted to see.
and i wanted to see you love me
the way i loved you

so i convinced myself you did
even though you didn't.

save your breath

do not tell me to get over
something that you have
no experience with.

explosive disaster

our love reminded me
of a firework.

when it first took off
it was explosive
and mesmerizing,
lighting up my life.

yet it quickly disappeared
leaving behind nothing
except for debris
and a pitch black sky.

we burned out.

ii.
thread

weightless

how am i meant to
love myself
when i feel unloved by those
who are meant to
love me the most?

there hasn't been a day
i can remember
or go back to
where i haven't felt like
a burden.
a weight.
a disappointment.

if i'm not even
enough for them
then how will i ever be
enough for myself?

empty

eyes that once held so much
purity
and innocence
eyes that used to be
big
and bold
eyes that were
bright
and held the future.

had become
baggy
and permanently red.

you could see right through them
you could look
all you wanted to.

but you would never find anything.

the life had been sucked out of them.

there was no longer
a soul behind them.

a different type of writer's block

writing has been my saving grace
for as long as i can remember
when i feel *anything*
i immediately resort
to my pen and paper.

it's the safest way of unleashing
the monsters clawing at my insides,
begging to escape
without causing harm to myself.

but i have days
where i'm too afraid to write.

because writing
means realizing.

because writing
means it's no longer
just inside my head
but now it's real.

i at times fear what i scribble down
or type out
will haunt me forever.

truth comes out at night

love is meant to change your life
for the better.

so why am i up at 3am
for the fourth time this week
trying to convince myself
i'm living a dream
rather than the same recurring nightmare
i face every day when i wake up?

helpless

you took away all of my abilities
you see i once knew how to
speak my mind
but you trained me to keep my
thoughts to myself
since they weren't worthy
of your time.

you see i once knew how to smile
a *genuine* smile
eyes and all
until you made it
near impossible to gather up
enough energy
to slightly turn up the
corners of my mouth.

you see i once knew how to
swim like a fish
until you consumed me with a wave
knocking me down
right in front of you
watching me drown.

you see i once knew how to
shower myself in self love
you quickly turned it into
self hate.
repeatedly telling me
i wasn't worth it
until i believed you.

a first for everything

true emptiness came to me
the day i asked you
why you loved me.

you struggled to answer
and i don't think you knew
i noticed.

i noticed
how your eyes began
darting around the room,
how your leg was
shaking back and forth
and the sheet of sweat
that covered your palms.

when you said
"i just do"
i knew you didn't
and i knew you were unsure.

it felt like getting stabbed
to be so sure of someone
who's unsure of you.

there was no worse pain than knowing
the one i had spent years loving,
who i had changed for,
the one i put above myself,
was still questioning my worth.

true emptiness came to me
6 months later
when i asked you
why you loved me.

you looked me straight in the eyes
and said you didn't
without even flinching.

it wasn't until later that night
while i laid awake
replaying the way it sounded
over and over.

how smooth it must have felt
coming through your lips
but how rough it sounded to me
like nails on a chalkboard.

i realized for the first time
you were finally sure of something.

storyteller

i remember all the stories you told me
of people from your past
i've never forgotten one.

i remember when you told me about
your first love as a child
how you always made sure to save her a swing
right next to you
how you would sneak an extra brownie
in your lunchbox
specifically to give to her
and how she made your insides
feel like jelly.

i remember the man from the train station
who returned your wallet
after you had dropped it
how you sat with him before departing
welcoming in any wisdom he had to offer
and before you went your separate ways
he told you,
"we become careless about life
when we're in a rush
for the wrong things."

i remember your best friend
the one you always found yourself
involved in mischief with
and how with both of your
imaginations combined
you could go anywhere you dreamed of
how you were each other's partner in crime
until he moved away in the summer of 2006

and you haven't had
a friend like him since.

one of my favorite past times
was falling into a state of relaxation
as your stories left your lips
making their way into my ears
bringing me a sense of comfort
like an old favorite song you haven't
heard in years.

i awaited each new story
like a child waiting for their parent
to read them the next chapter
of a book they dive into
every night before slumber.

little did i know
there would come a day
where i would no longer
hold a place in your life.

little did i know
one day
i would become
one of your stories.

sleepwalking

i started sleepwalking through life
left in a trance
stuck wondering
if this is living
why don't i feel alive?

each night i laid awake
wondering when the day would come
where i'd have the courage
to stop living for you
and stop being who you
wanted me to be.

each night i laid awake
wondering when the day would come
that instead of sleepwalking
i'd start dancing carelessly
and live life for me.

ear ringing silence

silence was no longer silence
it ironically became louder
than actual noise.

because in those meant-to-be
moments of silence
was when i'd hear it all.

the demons i've tried to
suffocate for years
would find a way to breathe
as if the silence
quenched them with air
the air i needed in my lungs
but was too far out of reach.

my eyes would not show me
the world in front of me
but instead the moments
that were engraved in my memory
despite how many packs of erasers
i went through in attempt to
pretend they never happened,
but you can't erase your reality
no matter how hard you try.

i could hear the screams,
my screams
that were begging to come out.

the ones i kept tied up with chains
and locked inside
refusing to let them out.

because if they were out
no one would care to listen
and i'd only be left
with a scratched throat
and tear stained face
even though i always kept
a spare key in my pocket
just incase one day
i'd find the courage to fight against
what my life had become.

but it didn't matter
how tight the chains were
it didn't matter
how unwilling i was to unleash it all
they knew how to unlock themselves
during the dreaded
avoided silence.

the power of nothing

how exhausting it is
to feel nothing.
almost as if nothing
had become
everything
all at once.

worst enemy

anxiety is having someone who is absolutely against you living inside your mind. it's non stop wondering of am i pushing everyone out of my life because they are toxic or because my anxiety is forcing me to do so? leaving you constantly stuck between the thought of am i choosing to be on my own because they are not what i need in my life or because my anxiety is trying to prove i'm not good enough to be in theirs? which eventually leads you to turning against your own self, only capable of listening to the anxiety as it has become all you know, it's the only thing you are familiar with and you live off of familiarity since you find comfort in it. comfort makes you feel sure about yourself even when you know the anxiety is wrong. it's an ongoing cycle of persuading you to not believe in yourself, no matter how bad you know you need to.

to all boys and men who suffer from mental illness

do not be discouraged
by days where you break down
from not being able to
handle one more second.

do not be afraid to *feel*
let your emotions in
and release them in whichever way
best helps you.

because while the world is busy
labeling you as weak
and unmanly
for enduring pain they have never
came close to experiencing,

you are being warriors.

my anxiety's visage

my anxiety makes me believe
that i am unwanted
and worthless
that one day
no one will be by my side.

because why would anyone
want someone like me
in their life?

instead of showing me the opposite
or proving the anxiety wrong
you fed into it.

and suddenly, my anxiety
had a face.

lifeless

i have become so afraid
of living life
the "wrong" way.

that in turn
i am not even living
at all.

echo

the words of my anxiety could be anything. whether they were telling me i should give up already, that i am not strong enough, or that i am a burden on everyone's life. i could hear how i am worthless, how people are only in my life out of pity, or that things would be better off if i wasn't alive. i'd hear all of that at once. if i even attempted to block out those words, they'd get louder. they'd play over and over until i had no choice, but to listen. until i stopped trying to fight them off. until i believed them. when i'd try to take another breath, in the back of my mind i'd think, "what's the point?". the words made me feel so little, so weak, that i was blinded from how strong i was for enduring what i did every single night.

cons of being a believer

my problem has always been
i believe too much.

i believe in seeing the good in others
no matter what they have done to me
i believe that people will keep their promises
regardless of how many they break
because "this time it'll be different"
even though i know it won't be
i'd rather believe my false hope
than face the reality
of you constantly lying to me.

i believe in second chances
and second chances to those
previously given chances
i believe in words and find comfort in them
when i'm told something,
i expect to receive it.

i believe the universe has a way of giving us
exactly what we need
with perfect timing
whether that being a lesson
or a lifetime lover.

i believed in you
so much
that i shape shifted my mind
to believe you would never hurt me
despite the fact you already were.

i believed in you

so much
that i stopped believing in myself.

tired

i am tired
but not just from
lack of sleep
that is reflected in my drooping eyes.

i am tired of trying
to explain myself to others
when they should be eager to help me
without needing an explanation.

i am tired of the ache in my chest
that makes it feel
near impossible
for just one more breath
to come through.

i am tired of questioning what i did
to deserve such a curse
that makes me feel as if
i'm from another planet
and do not belong.

i am tired
of being at war
with my mind.

celebrate the little victories

some days
just pulling together
the strength
to get out of bed is an
accomplishment.

and that is okay.

rainstorm

and all of a sudden it started raining,
completely pouring.

but not droplets from the sky above
instead it was because of me.

i was tired of the dark rain cloud
constantly following over me.

so instead of trying to avoid it
and walk around shielding myself
from the water i was sure
would eventually
drown me,

i let it flow out.

it engulfed every last
toxic piece of me
and went its own route
drizzling down my skin
leaving behind a feeling of
refreshment
and renewal.

i accepted what had happened to me.
i chose to finally
face my fears
instead of running in the
opposite direction.
i separated past from present and future.
i decided to rise against and fight
what i used to let consume me

no matter how long it may take.
i will be patient.
i let the negativity wash away.

choose you

to leave a toxic relationship
you must understand
you are not giving up on them,
but rather accepting the fact
they have already given up on you.

you are not going back
on the promises you made,
but rather opening your eyes
to the fact they never kept one.

you are not in the wrong
for no longer feeding unconditional love
into someone who couldn't do in a year
what you would do for them
in a day.

you are not in the wrong
for choosing you.

don't be food for his ego

changing yourself will never
make him love you.

it will only make him
fall in love with his ego more
knowing he can
mold you like clay
into whoever he wants you to be
the version of you
that is not truly
you.

if rearranging yourself
to fit his standards
is the only possible way
to make him love you
then he never deserved a chance to love
the *real* you
to begin with.

i never needed you

i was so overwhelmed by what i thought was love you were consuming me with, i never had time to stop and realize i wasn't swimming in your love, but rather drowning in your shadow. if i were to be asked about our love back then, my face would light up and i could have gone on for hours. now the sound of your name drains the color out of my once glowing face and leaves me feeling empty.

i never had time to stop and realize you never even loved me, not in the slightest. instead you loved the idea of being loved. you loved how for once, you didn't feel so alone. you loved how easily you could take advantage of me, and i let you because i was certain love meant making sacrifices, no matter how much they hurt. no matter how many tears i let out. no matter how little i meant to you. you were selfish and had an obsession with only taking your feelings into consideration. my unconditional love made you feel as if you could fly to the moon, but you forgot to take me with you.

you had me convinced i needed you. that i would be nowhere in life if it wasn't for you. that without you, i'd be nothing. to appear bigger you made me feel small. to ignore your flaws you constantly pointed out mine. to fix yourself you destroyed me.

in reality, i did not need you.

you needed me.

unwelcome

you expect me
to wait for you
when you leave me stranded.

you expect me
to have my arms
wide open
welcoming you home.

you have overstayed
your visit
and are welcome
no more.

everlasting garden

do not give him
the benefit of the doubt
if he has hurt you in a way
you wouldn't dare
wish upon anyone else,
in a way that sends chills down your spine,
in a way that makes your body tense,
he will do it again.

he will do it until it is all you know.
he will do it until you make excuses for him.
he will do it until you blame yourself.

do not give him a pathway to step on your heart
and walk all over it
as if it's nothing but
dead weeds.

because you are an everlasting garden
with flowers sprouting in a
variety of colors
if you continue to let him
walk all over you
and rip you from your roots
how do you ever expect to grow?

the fall before the rise

one will first
fall
before having the ability
to build themselves up
into their full potential.

you are a home

have the strength to stop letting people
walk in and out of your life
as they please.

you deserve someone
who sees you as a home
who wants to be there
for all of your Sunday mornings
and midnight rambles.

not someone
who sees you as a hotel
only using you
when they need somewhere
to unload their baggage
and sleep.

the advice i was never given

do not lose yourself while loving someone else. do not fall for someone's potential. what you see is what you get. and that is *all* you will get. do not lose sleep wondering why you aren't enough for someone. you are more than that. do not be so busy trying to force someone to love you that you forget to love yourself. do not think things will change if they haven't already. do not think you need anyone other than yourself. do not settle out of fear of never finding anyone else to love you. do not change who you are for someone who can't even be bothered to ask how your day went. do not stick around for someone you're constantly begging to receive the slightest bit of affection from. do not view yourself as a handful just because someone is not strong enough to hold all the love you have to offer.

because the truth is, the right person won't feel like work. the right person won't have you losing sleep from questioning your worth. they won't need a reminder to love you how you love them. they won't make you feel like a burden for simply caring. they won't constantly bring you down, but instead up with them. they won't run away when things get slightly difficult. they will ask about you so much that you'll get tired of talking about yourself, but that's their favorite part of the day. they won't make you scared of love. instead they will have you wanting more. they will have you wondering why you ever settled. they will make you realize why it never worked with anyone else.

lock up

stop keeping your door unlocked
for someone who never
comes home.

mountain mover

you deserve someone
who would move mountains
and swim across oceans
to be with you.

learn to distinguish them
from someone who instead
pushes the mountains
in front of you
or drowns you
in their oceans
of artificial love.

unpack yourself

it is okay to have days
where you feel imprisoned
by your own bedroom walls.

it is okay to have days
where you can barely
pick your own self up.

you have stowed away
all of your feelings
deep inside
as you do with
old belongings
into the attic.

but your feelings deserve days
where they can be
sprawled out
instead of stacked
on an already packed shelf.

because after all
feelings are meant
to be felt.

light

i've never really agreed
with saying someone
gave you light in your life
and that without them
you would have none.

because you see
they did not bring you
that light.

it's been there
all along
and always will be.

they just showed you
where to find it.

human

i do not like
being called "broken".
when something breaks
you throw it in the trash
because it no longer works.

i do not belong in the trash
i still work
i'm fighting harder than ever before.

just because someone is not
at the highest point in their life
does not give us the right
to refer to them as broken.
if that were the case
we would all be broken
seeing as no one has yet
figured life out.

struggling and experiencing pain
along with hardships and failure
does not make us broken
it makes us human.

balance

maybe there is a reason
to why bad things happen to us
maybe there is a reason to why some days
we cry until our bodies ache
and want nothing
but to be swallowed by the earth.

because if we didn't know sadness
how would we know the feeling
of being so happy
our cheeks hurt from smiling?

if we didn't know neglect
how would we know what it's like
to be cared for
and comforted in our worst possible state?

if we didn't know that
blood boiling sensation
that goes through us when we are
filled with anger
how would we know serenity?

you see
the good balances the bad
we need one
to have knowledge of the other.

we should never feel stupid
or put off by our emotions

embrace them
learn from them.

you've gone through so much
and you are stronger than ever.

so instead of constantly wondering
why bad things happen to you
first realize
without that feeling of being
pushed away
by the wrong person
you wouldn't know what it's like
to be pulled in closer
by the right person.

without that feeling of
heartbreak
you wouldn't know that breath of relief
when you realize you have finally
moved on.

you wouldn't know what it's like
to experience real love
the kind you always deserved.

be thankful for your bad times
because they show you your value
and how much you deserve.

and believe me when i say
you deserve it all.

you know yourself best

you know what is best for you. you know what you want. you know what will help you. you know what is healthy for you. you were your first friend. you were your first shoulder to cry on. you know what the voices are saying inside your head when you can't sleep. you picked yourself up every time you fell down. you are capable of achieving anything you set your mind to. you know your weaknesses just as much as you know your strengths. you know yourself more than anyone else in this world knows you. do not let anyone ever convince you otherwise.

your feelings matter

no matter how much
you love someone
no one deserves a free pass
for hurting you.

timekeeper's retire

i will not wait around
like your personal clock
ticking as the seconds go by
having no point in life
but to count the seconds
of your absence.

my own

you cannot claim me as yours
when all you do
is use me and
show me off
like an object
rather than the masterpiece
of a human being
that i am.

you cannot claim me as yours
when all you do
is walk over me
like the mat
placed before the front door.

you cannot claim me as yours
when at the times that
people aren't looking
your attention is focused
on lusting over other women
that you intend to have
take my place.

i am not your property
i belong to nobody
except myself.

iii.
mend

alleviate your pain

the one
who has gone through
so much pain
is also the one
who spends their time
helping others heal.

it's time to heal yourself.

my life

i was not given a mouth
to speak the words you wish to hear
not caring how bitter
they taste to me
or how much regret lives inside of them.

i was not given eyes
to view my future solely from
your point of view
leaving me with no choice
but to become blind
to what i really wanted my vision set on.

i was not given ears
to hear the spiteful words
you aim directly at me
without even noticing how sharp they are
and how much damage they do.

i was not given this life
only to constantly be convinced
it isn't mine to live.

labels

suffering from a
mental illness
does not make me crazy
or a freak
it does not make me pathetic
or attention seeking
it does not make me broken
or lost
it does not make me inadequate
or useless
it does not make me "too sensitive"
or "not worth it".

labels go on inanimate objects
and things that do not have
a beating heart
they do not belong
on human beings.

suffering from a
mental illness
makes me in need of
proper help and care
love and support.

give me that
instead of a label.

heart of gold

you would think
after all the tears i've shed
the countless times i've been lied to
the ways i've been belittled
how useless i've been made
to be seen by others
that my heart would be like stone.

rock solid,
cold,
colorless,
lifeless.

yet my heart has managed
to remain gold
full of pure intentions
and never ending
love for others.

persuasion

my whole life
i was reminded by you
how i am not enough.

that i am a waste of space
i am nothing.

and i believed you.

i'm not as easily persuaded anymore.

elixir

a toxic relationship
will make you feel
as if you are
the poison.

i hope you maintain enough
self worth
to look yourself in the mirror
and see that you
are the elixir.

i am not my mental illness

my anxiety is pushing others out of my life
to leave me feeling isolated
as if i brought it all upon myself.

my anxiety is leaving me with no energy
on some days not even enough
to wish things were different,
on some days not even enough
to ask what i did to deserve
a mind that is completely against me.

my anxiety is what convinces me
there is not one trace of beauty when it comes
to who i am
its logic being, how could someone with such
an ugly disorder
ever be seen as beautiful?

i am putting in every ounce of effort
to maintain relationships with
those who i surround myself with
because i am nowhere near a burden to them
despite what my anxiety wants me to believe.

i am the one who finds motivation
to get out of bed in the morning,
despite how terrible the previous night was
because i have more strength than
my worst nightmares
that i am currently living.

i am who i see looking right back at myself
when i stare into the mirror

as i remind myself,

that yes
my mental illness
is ripping me away
from my loved ones
and even myself.

that yes
my mental illness
strips me of
any thought that consists
of believing in myself.

that yes
my mental illness is
ugly and horrendous.

but *i* am not to be viewed as a fake friend
or someone who is told they
"always ditch out on plans".

but *i* am not weak
i have the weight of the world
crushing on my shoulders
yet am still finding a way to stand.

but *i* am not ugly
for having something i never asked for
for something i put in all my effort
to control.
and how is that courage i hold
not to be seen as
beautiful?

and *i* most definitely
am not
my mental illness.

fresh air

the thought of being in a
room by myself
used to terrify me.

being alone meant hearing my thoughts
it didn't matter how loud
i turned up the music
my mind was more powerful
it knew all the nooks and crannies
and exactly how to get into them.

i realized i devoted all my strength
toward muting my mind
that i became weak elsewhere.

each and every thought
had to be silenced
as i refused to hear what they entailed
i took away my own voice
without even realizing it.
i was suffocating myself.

giving the thoughts no other option
but to build up
and break out
in ways that would drain me.

i now find myself
choosing to turn the music off
because i'd rather hear what's going on
inside my head.

i learned to let myself breathe.

why i write

i write to say the things
others are too afraid
to speak of out loud.

i write to put the problems
people have difficulty explaining
onto paper.

i write to give my mind a break
from the nonstop thoughts
flowing in and out at full speed
because it at times feels like
i do not have enough strength
to think.

i write to create
something out of nothing
that could stick with someone
forever
and change their life.

i write to show others
they aren't alone.

i write to fill the silence.

the power of words

words are as
powerful
as a knife.

they have the
ability to sting.

but
they can also heal.

choose how you use yours
wisely.

slipped right through you

you made it seem like
losing me
was the last thing you intended to happen
that you fought as hard
and long as possible
to keep me in your life.

like every last excruciating second
was spent in fulfilling
your broken promises
and treating me how
i deserved to be treated
and how i should've been treated
all along.

when really
it was only me fighting
it was me having to make up for
your lack of effort.

while you were too busy
convincing yourself that
you weren't hurting me
you let me slip
right through your fingers.

your biggest flaw

you never realized
i was willing to do
anything for you.

you wanted me to be
your own creation
of what you envisioned
your perfect match to be
even if who that was
wasn't me
because who i already was
wasn't good enough for you.

so i'd let you pick me apart
and you rearranged the pieces of me
placing them where you wanted
as if i was a puzzle.
except you were jamming the pieces
where they didn't fit or belong
regardless of how much i cried
when i'd tell you i can no longer recognize
the girl staring back at me in the mirror.

but you'd reassure me by telling me,
"now you're perfect",
"now you're who i want".

and if i was who you wanted
nothing else mattered.

you never realized
i was willing to do
anything for you.

i began taking the blame
for all your wrongdoings
because convincing myself that the reason
everything was falling apart
was because of me
was a hell of a lot easier
than facing the wrath you would
unleash unto me
for pointing out one of your flaws.

it had become clear you viewed me
as less than you
in your eyes i was incapable of doing anything
even though i was
the glue holding us together
it had become easier for you to convince me
i was a problem
instead of owning up to all the problems
you were causing.

and i allowed you to
because love means making sacrifices
it wasn't until later i learned
those sacrifices
aren't meant to break you.

you never realized
i was willing to do
anything for you.

but i was too busy trying to
have you love me
the way i loved you
i was oblivious to the fact
real love shouldn't have me up

each and every night
wondering when it would end.

real love shouldn't have me questioning
why i will never
be enough for you.

real love shouldn't have me
feeling more lonely
than i ever have
in my entire life.

it wasn't until i realized
you only loved how i loved you
and how my love made you feel.

you felt invincible
you felt on top of the world
you were so high on my love
that it never even crossed your mind
to take a second and see
you were destroying me.

ghostly presence

i hope every time you listen to
that song i showed you
on the road trip we took last fall
all you can hear is me
babbling on and on
about why i connect with it so deeply.

i hope when you watch
my favorite movie
you feel my presence right next to you
spread out on the couch
and see me bundled up in a blanket,
eyes fixed on the television.

i hope when you eat
a scoop of ice cream
at two in the morning
you see me sitting across the table
saying how a good night's sleep is dependent
on a late night snack.

i hope i continue to fill
all the cracks in your life.

jen's

i gave you my trust
even though i only had
a little to spare,
yet somehow
you destroyed it all
without having any care.
i told you my story
and named
all my fears
you made me relive them
as if you didn't
even hear.

i came to you
for one thing,
that thing being love.
i made you my priority
nothing else mattered,
because you were above.

it wasn't reciprocated
not even one bit
and i was left there
to only feel hated
not just by you
but by my own self.

i hated it all
how much i give,
how deeply i love,
how quickly i fall.

that's when i realized

what i had wasn't a flaw
i have a big heart
and it's a privilege
i should've realized
this from the start.

you're the one
who is left
with a loss
because a heart like mine
is something you'll never ever
again come across.

full

i knew i no longer loved you
when you came to me
eager to shower me in
fake love
and broken promises
only to use me
for your own good once more
you expected me to open the door
welcoming you home.

i am no longer
blinded by your lies
i did not feel full from your affection
but rather empty.

and as i shut the door
i felt like i could
breathe again
knowing i was no longer
going to let you drain me.

warriors

how comforting it is to realize
our current battles result in armor
only making us stronger
allowing us to conquer
the next obstacle with ease.

choose your fate

although we cannot choose
the bad things that happen to us
we *can* choose
how we react to them
and morph them into something
beneficial to us.

reason

maybe we're all just looking
for a reason.
a reason to wake up,
a reason to get through another day,
a reason to breathe.

but we find the answer
in the wrong places.

your reason to breathe is not
to continuously try to be
who you are not
solely to impress those people
who you've always wanted to be friends with.

your reason to breathe is not
to live a life you don't want
out of fear of going after
what you really desire.

your reason to breathe is not
to blame yourself for all the difficulties
currently happening in your life.

your reason to breathe
is to one day look back on yourself
and realize you made it
because you were the reason
all along.

after rain comes a rainbow

your life has yet
to be lived through fully
challenges will arise
that you have not yet dealt with
and failure will happen.

don't look down
on your failure
like a dark rain cloud
pouring on your sunny day.

but instead
see it as an experience
and let each be seen
as a healing type of rain
falling into your soil
helping you grow stronger
allowing you
to fully blossom
and see the rainbow.

feel

let it out
scream so loud
that your throat feels like
a scratched record.

pour out all the tears
that have been forming inside
waiting to burst through.

scribble your thoughts
the ones you
don't dare say out loud
onto paper
and ignite it
watch it burn.

let it out
but don't ever beat yourself up
for feeling.

you are strength

you are not your mental illness
you are not the endless tears
but instead the courageous hand
that wipes them away.

you are not the ache in your chest
but instead the breaths
you keep pushing out
no matter how shaky they are.

you are not the voice in your head
telling you to give up
but instead the triumphant one
that tells you to keep going.

you are not your mental illness
you are strength
say those words to yourself
believe them.

sprout

no one can fix you
because you are not broken.

instead of constantly searching
for unneeded pieces
to fill what you view
as emptiness
start to water the parts of you
that are yearning to blossom.

the ones you have never
brought into the light
acknowledge that you are growing
and continuing to find yourself
day by day.

recognize that you are capable
of sprouting into the person
you want to be
and then you will realize
how full you are.

self love

self love is the most
important of all
so that no matter what
you always have someone
to pick you up
when you fall.

preserve your water

if they no longer
accept you
move forward.

do not waste your time
watering a garden
that is already dead.

blossom

you came into my life
during a time when i was buried
deep below the ground
i had been stomped on
and left to wither away.

you immediately made me yours
showering me with kisses
quenching my thirst for love
bringing light into my life
that i had not seen for ages.

soon enough,
i blossomed.

all because of you,
i felt beautiful again.

until one day
you dug me out of the ground
and although at the time
i felt wanted
i did not know
you were slowly killing me
as i could not go on
without my roots.

you no longer wanted me
as i was now not able to fulfill
your selfish needs.

i thought i would never
see light once more

but i began to grow
faster than ever before.

i flourished
i stood tall
and that is when i realized
i never needed you
to show me my own beauty
or make me feel loved
all i need is myself.

as with or without you
i am the same
and i am beautiful.

release

i do not wish
bad things upon anyone.

if someone is no longer
involved in my life
it was meant to be that way
my time will not be spent
wishing the worst upon them.

they brought about
new experiences
and showed me life
from a different perspective.

i will not be bitter
because in the end
the only one that will cause
any harm to
is myself.

you are not alone

this is your reminder that you are not alone. you are not a freak for your problems. you are not helpless. you are not a lost cause. close your eyes. take a breath. breathe in. breathe out. you have the strength needed to overcome your fight. it might not seem like it is always there, but it is. do not give up if your problems are not solved in one day. with constant determination, you will notice change. it will happen. you are human. you are important. you will get through the day. you can do this. i believe in you. i am rooting for you. it is time to start rooting for yourself.

staying afloat

i spent so much of my time
wishing things were different
i failed to realized
maybe they were meant to work out
exactly in this way.

i've experienced cruelty and hatred
from those meant to love me most
and although it tore me apart
and ripped me to shreds
it shaped me into the most selfless being
inspiring me to want to be
nothing but loving
to those around me
it helped me see my worth
and wow,
i am worth way more
than they ever said i did.

i've experienced downfall and failure
over
and over again
to the point where i questioned
why i even kept trying
i'm glad i never let
the what seemed to be
impossible weight of doubt
keep me down
allowing me to fully realize
how strong i truly am.

i've experienced loss
loss of love

not only from others
but myself as well
loss of people who i could have never
predicted myself losing
loss of hope
loss of motivation
yet somehow,
while losing
i was gaining.
i was gaining confirmation
of who really meant it
when they said they'd stay
aside from who just said it
to trick me into loving them
how i was aching to be loved.

at the end of the day
no matter how odd it may sound
i am thankful for my hardships
and i now laugh at them.

they thought they could break me
and although it sure
felt like they did when i faced them
i overcame each and every one of my battles
it doesn't matter if i came out
barely able to breathe
with a fire in my chest
and tear stained cheeks,
it doesn't matter if i had to reteach myself
a few things here and there,
it doesn't matter if i lost myself
because i eventually found myself
the strongest version of myself.

none of these things take away
from how hard i fought
or how many times i picked myself up
even when it felt like i had
forgotten how to walk
none of these things take away
from the fact that i made it.

the journey isn't simple
it is never going to be smooth sailing
but the harsh waves make you
you.

you'll feel like you're drowning
but it's in those moments
where you look at what's pulling you underwater
straight in the face
and show it how well you can swim.

once you look back on
how far you've already swam
on the tsunamis you've made it through
you'll see that nothing
holds the power to break you.

reservation for one

learn to spend time
with yourself
in a way that you look forward to
rather than only having it
be consumed of stressful moments
rather than it only being when work
needs to be done.

instead of ordering take out
get dressed up
and make reservations for one
at your favorite restaurant.

do not let the beautiful weather
go to waste
sit outside and let your skin
soak up the sun
while you play your favorite songs
and eat your favorite fruit.

take a break from the nights out
to instead rent a movie
you've never seen
and make a bowl of popcorn
for you to sit and enjoy.

take time to get to know yourself
your quirks and your habits
your strengths and weaknesses
reward yourself for how far you've come
fall in love with who you are.

stopwatch

time is limited
and yours deserves to be valued
do not waste yours
on someone who can't be bothered
to give you a minute of theirs.

complete

i do not need
to be completed
by someone else.

i am my own puzzle
my own
finished painting.

real

wear your hair
messy
from the previous night's sleep.

go out with your face untouched
letting it glow
from sunlight.

pick out the outfit
in the back of your closet
you never had the guts
to put on.

don't be afraid,
be you.

power of one

allow yourself to realize
another human does not
and will not
ever hold the power
to destroy you.

you are whole
you are complete.

any person you encounter
is just someone
to teach you another one
of life's lessons.

do not let yourself believe
that you are empty
but with them you are full
or else you will only be
destroying yourself.

to all women

enough assuming you know
the intentions of another
just from one glance.
enough tearing one another apart
like a sheet of paper
ripping each other to pieces.
enough placing men above yourselves
letting them be viewed as a trophy
while you fight over them relentlessly.
enough seeing other women
as competition against you
when you've both yet to speak a word to the other.

more joining together in strength
to become unbreakable
against those who belittle us.
more open mindedness
give someone a chance to express themselves
before judging them by appearance.
more teamwork with those you encounter
to lift each other's spirits
and take over the world.

free will

if you choose
to leave my life
i will no longer beg you to stay.

i deserve to be
appreciated.

not walked out on.

shine

there's nothing wrong
with being selfish
selfishness can be a good thing,
if it's the right kind.

take time for yourself
even if it makes you five minutes late.

say what's on your mind
no matter how scared you are.

cut out the people
who don't deserve a spot in your life.

learn to be in love with yourself
more than anyone else.

have courage to say "no"
to the things you do not want to do.

stop making excuses for others.

put yourself first
always
and watch how you'll shine.

permanent

i am me
no more
or less.

simply me.

you either take me
for who i am
or watch
as someone else does so.

i will not change
to fit your standards.

favorite tee

you'll get worn out
while existing
just like your
favorite t-shirt
that is becoming
unhemmed
and has a small hole
where your left shoulder is.

but despite the damage
it is still
your favorite.

first choice

you cannot put me
on a shelf
left to collect dust
and pick me up
as you please.

i am not
a place holder
or a last resort.

new year

i do not go into a new year
saying "please be kind to me"
because i have learned
the world does not care
about what you beg for.

the world is not always kind
it will continuously knock you down
to the point where it feels like
you've forgotten how to walk.

but it's up to you
will you stay on the ground
or teach your legs how to work
once more?

will you follow your words with actions
or just say them and simply forget?

so dear new year,
it does not matter
if you are kind to me
or not
as i will still do what i need to get done
and be the person
i've always wanted to become.

regret

i don't believe in regrets
whether it's something as small
as that dress i bought in 10th grade
that i wouldn't be caught dead
wearing now
or the way i used to apply my eyeliner
so thick you could barely
see my eyes.

not even something as big
as forcing a friendship
i knew i no longer wanted
or falling for you
only to not be caught.

because at one point
it was everything i wanted
my heart was set on it
and i found happiness
within that moment
within those people
within the feelings.

so if you had to ask me
the answer is no
i do not have any regrets
only experiences
that i learned from.

masterpiece

i am art
i deserve to be
displayed on the wall
in the center of your living room
right where the sunlight
directly hits every afternoon.

not stored away in your basement
as you take the time
to decide whether or not
i fit your taste.

his sunset

he viewed me as a sunset
as i enlightened him
with my colors.

the deep reds reminding him
of the scars from his past
the bright yellows being the light
he is still learning to let in
the mysterious purples
intriguing his urge
to discover who i am.

i showed him that beauty can be found
in the simplest of things
and can be taken from
the palm of his hand
before he even realizes it
teaching him to appreciate
the time he has with someone
as time is limited
and you never truly know
how much you have left.

he viewed me as a sunset
that came in a time of dusk
illuminating his life
and then vanishing
right before his eyes.

just like the bittersweet feeling
of an almost lover.

refreshment

you bring a refreshing feeling into my life. it reminds me of the shower i took at two a.m. last night, as i washed the day away. bringing about a new start. when i crawled into my freshly washed sheets that gave off an aroma of cleanliness i couldn't stop the flood of thoughts about you which quickly entered my mind. the deep breath i took to relax my body reminded me of how calming it feels just to be in your presence. you're a break from the madness. you're fresh air for my lungs. you're what it feels like to breathe again.

enough

the key is to find someone
who doesn't make you feel as if you need them
who realizes you put yourself
before anyone else
who recognizes how strong you are
on your own
who doesn't belittle you
or say "without me
you have nothing".

because they've seen how
powerful you are solo
they recognize your worth
to them
you're already enough.

awe

you make the littlest things
appear to be the most wonderful
i could spend hours
listening to your thoughts.

you amaze me
in every possible way
without even knowing it.

toxic relationships

stop excusing toxic relationships for love. letting someone overpower your self worth with their own is not love. constantly avoiding bringing up what bothers you and makes you uncomfortable because you fear the argument that will follow after is not love. feeling as if you are always walking on thin ice and dedicating your life to pleasing somebody else is not love. forgiving the same mistakes over and over again, even though the damage of them is physically and mentally draining you, is not love. sticking around while someone figures out how to treat you is not love. blaming yourself for the pain they are causing you because you do not want them feeling guilty is not love.

it is not your fault.

it is not your fault that they are unable to love you the way you love them. it has nothing to do with the value you hold as a person. it is not your fault that they have endured a rough past and attached to you because they saw how much love you have to offer. it is not your responsibility to mend somebody else. it is not your responsibility to wait around while somebody else gets themselves together. it is not your fault for wanting to receive the same effort back that you are putting in. it is not your fault for wanting more.

your love is not measured by how many punches you can take.

your love is not measured by how many times you will forgive the same mistakes.

your love is not measured by the amount of times you put your mental health aside in order to help theirs.

your love is not measured by the height of the pedestal you put them on while leaving yourself at the bottom.

you are not the toxic one. it doesn't matter how many times they try to tell you that you are.

you. are. not.

do not feel guilty for realizing you deserve better. do not let them tell you, "if you loved me like you said you did, then you would wait for me to get better". do not let them drag you down with them. do not let them belittle you by saying you won't find anyone else. do not allow someone to hold so much power over you that you have no control over your own actions. and do not ever let someone tell you what you want. you know yourself more than anyone.

trust yourself.

love yourself.

you're never overdue

when my lungs
feel as if there is no air
left inside
you fill me up with your love
allowing me to breathe.

when my head
feels as if it will explode
any second
from the amount of movement
going on inside
you place your lips
gently against my forehead
immediately sending a signal
throughout my being
telling me i am okay.

when my hands
shake so much
that it feels as if
i am a human earthquake
you take hold of them
and remind me
you are
and always will be
here for me.

i hope you stay forever.

medicine

put the hammer down
stop adding boards and nails
to the wall you are encapsulating yourself in
in hopes of pushing me away.

i will not hurt you
how they did
i intend to heal.

focus on the kindness in my eyes
the softness in my touch
my voice smooth as silk.

i am not someone from your past
and i do not intend
to one day become
someone from your past.

i am right here
and i am choosing
to stay.

red rose

you saw a side of me
i have never dared to give
anyone else.

a raw,
real side.

it consisted of my rants
when i couldn't sleep
and although they may have seemed
to be about the most
meaningless things
i had a reason for them.

i filled the air with noise
and non stop conversation
out of fear that if i were to be quiet
if we were to soak in the silence
that my deepest secrets
would somehow
unfold.

i feared you'd be able to
count my breaths
and read my unnerving body language
as you would quickly see
i'm not always as confident
as i deem to be.

you would pick up on how
nervous of a person
i actually am
how the textured pattern on my lips

wasn't from them being chapped
but because of my constant
biting down on them
to prevent myself
from letting too much
slip out.

little did i know
you picked up on these
habits of mine
ever since the first day we met
but you did not view them
in the way i did.

instead
you saw something in me
that i was eager for the rest of the world
to see in me.

you saw how badly i wanted to live
not just by getting by
but by standing out.

you saw the ball of fire that
sat in my chest
as i awaited the day where
i'd have enough courage
to push it out
and live with so much passion
that it would scare others.

you saw the desire i held
to prove myself
you saw it in me before
i saw it in myself

you saw it in me
until you taught me
how to see it in myself.

if there was a way to make
wishes come true
i'd wish for you to pour
the same amount of
overflowing love
you put into my life
similar to the cup of coffee you
overfill on a Monday morning
into your own.

it's funny how i always thought
i was one of the only people
who becomes so focused
on bringing comfort
into the lives of others
that i at times forget to find it
within myself
my heart was certain there would
never be another
to match mine.

until i met you.

i hope you learn to love who you are
as you should be
more than comfortable
with your true self
the one i was lucky enough to watch you
grow into.

i'd wish for you to understand

you are only human
just as you would always tell me
i hope you remove the microscope
in which you are always
putting yourself under
as you pick and pull at each
and every one of your flaws
so much that you fail to realize
how those flaws
aren't really flaws
but rather unique little qualities
that make you
you.

i'd wish for you to see how
perfect
you really are
i'd wish for you to see
in yourself,
what you saw in me.

my true love

my priorities were in the
wrong place
for some reason i was so set
on the idea
of finding love.

if someone loved me
i would feel wanted,
i would have a purpose,
i would be important.

if someone loved me
i wouldn't have to do it myself
especially since i was
emotionally unable to.

my obsession with
wanting to be wanted
had become so overwhelming
that i settled for
whatever i could take.

no matter how toxic it was
even if it stung my entire being,
even if it felt wrong,
even if it made me hate myself.

years passed until i grew
strong enough
to see my self worth.

i will no longer settle for
half given love

or blame myself
for someone's inability to give me
what i deserve.
there is no one on this planet
who can love me
more than i can love myself.

i was so set on the idea of
finding love
i failed to see it was right inside of me
the entire time
and if anyone deserves
unconditional love
it's me.

stay sweet

it is so important to remember
when you are going through
a wretched heartbreak
to not become
your bitterness,
your sadness,
or your despair.

do not fill your body
with the toxic thoughts
that will only burn you
from the inside out.

feel all you need to feel
and let out the pain
that was done onto you
but do not become
what hurt you.

do not become
a dark,
stone cold heart
because the only way
to get back to where you once were
is to fill yourself with
the love that you lost
which can easily be found
within yourself.

live

i want to discover all the
beauty of the earth.

i want to watch the sunrise
from one side of the world
then travel to the other
to see the sunset
but observe how much differently
it fades from a new perspective.

i want to run through
fields of flowers
i want to swim in all
the deep waters of the world
and step foot on
every last inch of land.

i want to learn new languages
and ways of life
i want to see the stars glittering
and lighting up the night sky.

i want to see life
in every way possible.

manifestation

the easiest way to fail
is by believing the idea
that good things will come to you.

it is up to you
to work for them
to go after them
to never settle for less
to constantly be hungry
for success.

if you choose to wait
you will be wasting time
and opportunities
ones that you could have shaped
to manifest your own destiny.

escape

we all have something
that lets us escape
without really going anywhere.

something that fills your
soul with warmth
even on your coldest days
something that allows you to dream
without being asleep.

whatever your escape is
hold onto it
never let it go.

to my 10 year old self

keep writing. do not put that pen down. do not listen to those who make fun of you for spending your time reading. do not think your dream is any less than those wanting to be doctors and lawyers. do not listen to the people who will soon pester you on finding a "real job". do not care about the opinion of preteen boys who are intimidated by your intelligence. do not pretend to not know the answers in class. being smart is not reserved for men only. embrace your passion. do not let the world dim your light. and most importantly, do not give up.

fear

we cannot be successful
by filling our head
with wishes
and "what ifs".

we can only be successful
when we take steps
towards our dreams
to turn them into reality.

nothing is too far out of reach
if you are willing to
take the steps to get there
even one step is closer than
not going after what will fill you
not going after what drives you.

because instead you let fear
consume you
making your dream
stay only a dream.

for you

stop living how others
want you to
stop living to please your parents
stop living to impress your friends.

because in the end
it'll be just you
looking back on your life.

and when you realize
that you didn't live for you
you'll also realize
you didn't live at all.

future

"you're just a kid" they say
or "you're too young" as if
they are insults
as if my age takes away
my intelligence
or maturity.

what is wrong with the youth
caring about politics
the environment
racial issues
and equality?

what is wrong with the youth
speaking out
and wanting change?

a person's age does not make them blind
to the disgusting actions
going on in the world
a person's age does not make their words
of any less or more value.

after all
although i am young,
this is my future.

luna

even in the complete darkness
of the silent night
the moon still shines.

it does not get discouraged
by the lack of illumination
but instead
takes advantage of
the absence of light
to shine brighter than ever.

step one

people can motivate
and provide you
with the tools
to accomplish your
wildest dreams
to be who you have always
wanted to be
to put yourself first.

but in the end
it comes down to you.

so ask yourself,

are you ready to change?

team effort

i've learned to get rid of
any person in my life
who competes with me.

i do not befriend people
only to race against them.

passion

write so much
that at the end of the day
your hand aches
from gripping the pencil so tight.

sing so loud
that your neighbors can hear
but all they can do is smile
from the joy prevalent
in your voice.

draw so often
that every inch of your wall is covered
by all the work you've created
as you display it with confidence.

create something out of nothing
have your passion be so strong
it lights the world on fire.

i'm better

i'm better now. but that doesn't mean i don't have days where i fall apart. that doesn't mean i don't have days where i struggle to fall asleep. that doesn't mean i'm never allowed to mess up again. and i think that's a problem we all have.

when we've pulled ourselves out of a rut, we are so terrified of falling back into it. this fear almost makes it easier to fall back in. it halts us from living in the present. the amount of pressure we put on ourselves to be happy is in turn driving out the happiness on its own.

i'm better now. meaning this time around, i'll pick myself up when i crumble. i'll let my mind speak its thoughts on the days i lay wide awake, and i'll actually listen. i've recognized my life will be full of mistakes. but, i'm better now, i've learned that i'll only grow from them.

new reality

my days used to start
with me wishing for them
to be over
staying within the walls of my bedroom
had become all i knew,
all i wanted.

i did not care to interact with anyone
the anxiety of not being
enough for them
even in a simple conversation
was too much to bare.

aches went through my shoulders
leaving me weak and bruised
the never ending weight
i put on myself
was only getting heavier
with time.

sleep had become my motivation
because when i was asleep,
the voices weren't as loud,
the paranoia wasn't as real,
the world was quiet.

i now start my days with
a warm cup of mint tea
thoughts of how lucky i am
to be living the life i live
bounce through
my once boggled mind.

i now can't get enough of the sun
kissing my skin
rejuvenating me into the girl i once
wished to be.
the one i now am.

my days now consist
of the battery of my phone
running low
from the amount of times
i turn it on
to check the time
as i now wish for more
minutes in a day.

because for the first time
reality has become
better than any dream
i could ever imagine.

final mold

i'm grateful for everyone
who has been in and out of my life
whether they brought along
good or bad experiences.

because from them
i have learned new things,
i have seen different places,
i have realized my worth,
and come to terms
with the idea that
if someone wants to be in my life
they will show me through effort.

because of all of you
and how i handled your absences
i have shaped myself
into who i am today.

thank you.

you + mending

i have come to terms with the fact that i will always be learning. life itself is a learning process. no matter how old i am, how many heartbreaks i go through, obstacles i face, or triumphs i have, there will always be one more around the corner. life does not pause for anyone. life does not care if you were looking at your red faced reflection last night in the mirror, watching the tears stream out of your swollen eyes. life does not care if you are finally feeling like yourself after months of pretending to be someone else. life will continue to go on whether you are standing straight up on your feet or knocked down on the ground. so why continue to pretend like you have it all figured out? why continue to put a weight of pressure on yourself to have control over an unpredictable life? you don't need your life planned out by tomorrow morning. take it day by day. experience happiness. experience loss. experience failure. experience fear. experience strength. *truly* experience it all. wrap yourself in the warmth of each emotion until you feel whole and are onto the next. each day you are more yourself than you were yesterday. each day you are stitching up your past and sewing it into your future.

you aren't weak for feeling.

you aren't broken.

you're mending.

all my love

do what you will with this book. do whatever must be done while experiencing the emotions that my words give you. highlight the parts that hold the most meaning to you. let teardrops fall onto the pages you relate so deeply with you feel as if i pulled them from your heart.

reread the pages that spoke to you until the words are engraved in your mind. allow the corners of your mouth to turn upwards when you find a sense of comfort within me. pass it into the hands of someone who you know needs it.

this book is meant to inspire. this is meant to be your sign. this is meant to leave you wondering why you have not yet gone after the best for yourself. it is possible.

it may take years, it could take days. but you won't ever know until you start.

and once you get it, you'll wonder what took you so long.

breathe. inhale. exhale.

envision yourself where you have always wanted to be. what makes you so undeserving to not go after it? you deserve to live life to its full potential. you will never be alone because i will always be here rooting for you.

if anyone deserves happiness, it's you. believe that.

live with passion. live with love. live for you.

so, what are you waiting for?

with love,

christina valles xx

index

needle

thread

mend

acknowledgments

to my dad, thank you for introducing me to art and constantly nourishing my creative mindset. thank you for always reminding me to follow my dreams and for the non stop support. thank you for being the definition of a hardworking human, which in return inspired me to want to be the same. thank you for making me smile when it seemed impossible. thank you for believing in me.

to my mom, thank you for encouraging me to read ever since i was a little girl and being the reason why i never stopped. thank you for being my shoulder to cry on and for the late night conversations when we both couldn't sleep. thank you for pushing me.

to alex, sarah and nico, thank you for being my escape away from the madness without even realizing it. thank you for showing me what a real smile feels like and for making my stomach hurt from laughing so much. thank you for being reminders that i have a purpose in this world.

to ms. cook, thank you for taking the time to edit this book. thank you for implementing such a strong English/reading curriculum in 7th/8th grade that only grew my love for it even more. thank you for turning me into a better writer. thank you for encouraging me.

to my closest friends, thank you for supporting my decisions, no matter how impulsive they can be. thank you for always checking in on me, despite the amount of times i would disappear into my own little world. thank you for being the people i could run to when i was at my weakest.

to gabriel, thank you for never letting me settle. thank you for your honesty, no matter how much it may hurt at times, i am always beyond grateful for it. thank you for allowing me to realize i am worth so much more. thank you for sticking by my side through my most stressful moments, as well as my most peaceful ones. thank you for helping me realize my full potential.

to my first muse, i used to despise you for breaking my heart, but i now thank you. without you, this book would have never been born. i imagine you will now think twice before falling for an artist.

about the author

christina valles is a 19 year old writer who was born and raised under the sun in phoenix, arizona. she has been a fan of creating all her life, but using words to make something out of nothing has always stuck out the most. when not writing, you can find her watching Disney movies, painting, admiring the sunset, or of course, sat in bed reading. mending is her first published poetry book.

for more updates follow @christina.valles on instagram.

Made in the USA
San Bernardino, CA
23 September 2018